A Throwaway Kid
Rescued from Darkness

But ye are a chosen generation, a royal priesthood, an holy nation, a peculiar people; that ye should shew forth the praises of him who hath called you out of darkness into his marvellous light; (1 Peter 2:9)

Kathy Neff

Palmer Enterprises
Reflecting the Light of God's Word

A Throwaway Kid
Rescued from Darkness

ISBN: 0-9913483-8-9
Copyright © 2017 by Kathy Neff

Cover photograph by Suzanne Caris
Email: scarisphoto@gmail.com
Website: www.SuzanneCaris.com

Published by Palmer Enterprises
1971 Ellsworth Drive
Lakeside Marblehead, OH 43440 USA
Email: palmer2916@roadrunner.com

All Scripture quotations are taken from the King James Version of the Bible.

Some of the names of the people portrayed in this book have been changed to respect their privacy.

Book contents, cover, or parts thereof may not be reproduced in any form, stored in a retrieval system, or transmitted in any form by any means – electronic, mechanical, photocopy, recording or otherwise – without prior written permission of the publisher, except as provided by United States of America copyright law.

Contents

Acknowledgements 4

Dedication 5

Introduction 7

Part One

Chapter 1:
A Rough Beginning 11

Chapter 2:
Time to Grow Up 33

Part Two

Chapter 3:
Trust God 51

Chapter 4:
Sisters, Friends & Family 113

Chapter 5:
Be Made Whole 141

Acknowledgments

*Special recognition goes to
Pastor Harry Hunt and his wife Dawna
for their love, kindness, comfort,
encouragement and strength.
In addition, I would like to acknowledge
my friend Stan Harold, who is now with
the Lord, for his devotion to God
and to the Body of Christ.
It was through Stan that the Thursday
evening Bible studies in my home
came to fruition.
I am also very thankful for the gracious
love and support of Aaron, Bennie,
Breonna, Caleb, Charlie, Dave, Dylan,
Jake, Jim, Katie, Kenny, Kevin, Matthew,
Nathan, and Steve.
Finally, my deepest appreciation goes to
Kathy Palmer. I am extremely grateful
for her assistance and expertise in
publishing my testimony of the Lord Jesus
Christ. Without her help, this book would
not have been written.*

Dedication

Dedicated to

My Savior & Lord Jesus Christ,

The loving memory

Of my dear late husband Tom,

And my extraordinary sons,

John and Jim.

Introduction

The memories flood in as I turn the pages of *A Throwaway Kid* and recall the loneliness, humiliation, and devastating pain that haunted my childhood and young adult life. Then God Almighty broke me through the darkness and brought victory!

Though I wasn't aware of it in my early years, I now know that Jesus was with me through the entire journey, especially in my darkest, scariest times. He was in my past, He is in my present, and He assures me He will be in my future.

> *...I am with you always, even unto the end of the world. (Matthew 28:20b)*

> *...I will never leave thee nor forsake thee. (Hebrews 13:5b)*

I fall short sometimes, yet God is forgiving and faithful. I walk through valleys, but

Jesus holds my hand and takes me from the valley to the mountaintop. God is always present, and He continually demonstrates His power in my life.

The Lord is well able to rescue, redeem, and save the vilest sinner. The enemy of my soul tried to rob me of the ability to give and receive love; yet, God used it all as a testimony of His power!

I now have a beautiful intimacy with my Bridegroom, the Lord Jesus Christ. I long to be His vessel and a conduit of His love. I pray that my story will encourage you and powerfully reveal the astonishing love of God. He has redeemed me and given me a brand new life!

> *Therefore if any man be in Christ, he is a new creature: old things are passed away; behold, all things are become new. (2 Corinthians 5:17)*
>
> *...we are more than conquerors through him that loved us. (Romans 8:37b)*

Part One

Chapter One
A Rough Beginning

No child should be forced to endure constant rejection, neglect, and abuse. I was placed in the foster care system at birth, and numerous moves from place to place permeate my earliest childhood memories. I had no sense of belonging or security. One day I would empty my little suitcase, and then very soon I had to fill it back up again.

"It's time to go!"

There were so many foster home placements, I can't remember them all. "Come on, Kathy! It's time to go!" This scene played out

A Throwaway Kid

all too frequently. There were no expressions of love or affection. There was no mom to comfort and nurture me, no dad to protect and provide for me.

I quickly adapted to this unsettling routine of being transferred from house to house. It was part of my life. It was normal to be placed in one location for a few days and then moved to a different location. Early on, I accepted that this was just how it was.

I have no joyful childhood memories, no pleasant memories of holidays or birthday parties. I remember the beatings, the first incident of sexual molestation at five years old, the constant belittling and degradation from other kids and from adults. Even routine daily activities could escalate into horrific experiences.

"Swallow that food!"

When I was very young, I remember being plopped in a high chair. The food was being shoved in my mouth so fast that I

A Rough Beginning

couldn't swallow it quickly enough. My mouth was too full of food, and I was choking. "Kathy, swallow that food!"

Immediately following this shrill command, I received a severe blow across my face. I was hit violently, and it sent me and my high chair crashing into the refrigerator. Not long after that incident, my little suitcase was packed, and I was leaving again.

The next placement I recall, I was about three years old. The foster couple I'd been placed with had two little girls of their own. As the girls were playing with their dolls and doll clothes on one side of the driveway, I was playing on the opposite side of the driveway with what I considered to be my toys. I can vividly remember that my toys consisted of sticks and leaves; that's all I had to play with.

As I looked over at the girls, I wasn't jealous or angry. I felt no emotion at all, as I watched them play. I accepted this as normal. I didn't cry, I wasn't sad, and I wasn't mad. I didn't think, "Boy, I wish I had those dolls to play with." I accepted that the sticks and leaves were my toys.

"Stop crying!"

There were innumerable incidents of verbal and physical abuse, countless slaps to the face and punches to the head. "Stop crying! I didn't hit you that hard!" Of course, the more I tried to stop crying, the more I cried; and the more I cried, the more I was slapped and punched.

Some children suffer horrendous treatment at the hands of adults, whether it be their foster or biological parents. Abuse is also meted out by their peers. To illustrate the magnitude of child abuse in the United States, consider the following 2015 statistics from the National Children's Alliance.

National Statistics on Child Abuse
In 2015, an estimated 1,670 children died from abuse and neglect in the

United States.[1] In 2015, Children's Advocacy Centers around the country served more than 311,000[2] child victims of abuse, providing victim advocacy and support to these children and their families.

Nearly 700,000 children are abused in the U.S. annually. An estimated 683,000 children (unique incidents) were victims of abuse and neglect in 2015, the most recent year for which there is national data.

CPS protects more than 3 million children. Approximately 3.4 million children received an investigation or alternative response from child protective

---

[1] *All national child abuse statistics cited from U.S. Administration for Children & Families, Child Maltreatment 2015.*
https://www.acf.hhs.gov/cb/resource/child-maltreatment-2015

[2] *National Children's Alliance 2015 national statistics collected from Children's Advocacy Center members and available on the NCA website:*
http://www.nationalchildrensalliance.org/cac-statistics

services agencies. 2.3 million children received prevention services.

The youngest children were most vulnerable to maltreatment. Children in the first year of their life had the highest rate of victimization of 24.2 per 1,000 children in the national population of the same age.

Neglect is the most common form of maltreatment. Of the children who experienced maltreatment or abuse, three-quarters suffered neglect; 17.2% suffered physical abuse; and 8.4% suffered sexual abuse. (Some children are polyvictimized — they have suffered more than one form of maltreatment.)

About four out of five abusers are the victims' parents. A parent of the child victim was the perpetrator in 78.1% of substantiated cases of child maltreatment.

A Rough Beginning

"This was my reality."

At the time I was in the foster care system in the 1940s and 1950s, there were no child advocacy groups. I thought my life was "normal." I didn't wonder what it would be like to have a mom and dad who loved me. I thought I was experiencing a typical family life. This was my reality; it was all I knew.

When I was five years old, not even in school yet, one of my foster brothers was walking with me, and he decided we should take a shortcut down an alley. There was a new horror awaiting me in that alley.

My foster parents' son, who was 20 years old, sexually molested me. His actions were heartless and coldhearted. I was merely an object to satisfy his lust. I wasn't his little sister to be protected and nurtured. I was nothing to him, just a throwaway kid.

I was terrified that the molestation would continue and terrified that someone would find out. In addition to fear, I was ashamed, because I was constantly told,

"Kathy, you're worthless. You can't do anything right!" I couldn't go to anyone for help, since I was usually blamed for anything bad that happened.

The molestation by my 20-year-old foster brother continued; and I was also later molested by another of my foster parents' sons, who was 18 years old.

When I was seven, in yet another foster placement, while I was taking a bath, someone (I don't recall who it was) grabbed my hair, turned my head face-up toward the faucet, and then turned on the water. The water came out full-force, blasting violently onto my face. I gasped for air, gagging and screaming, as I tried to breathe. To this day, I can't wash my hair while taking a shower. It causes me to hyperventilate and have debilitating panic attacks.

The constant moves from house to house continued. When I was about nine, I thought to myself, "Maybe if I keep quiet, they won't hurt me, and I won't have to move again." I preferred to stay in the hell I knew than to go into a hell I didn't know. The unknown seemed much scarier; it might even be worse than where I was.

So, I kept my mouth shut. Because I remained silent and stayed in the background as much as possible, I wasn't moved again. I was able to stay in my last foster home from age nine until I left the foster care system at sixteen. This would prove to be more of a curse than a blessing.

"Honor thy father and mother."

While in what would be my final foster home, one day I forgot to do one of my chores. My foster mother made me write every day for weeks, "I will honor my father and mother."

When I came home from school each day, my schedule consisted of doing my chores and homework, and then writing over and over, "I will honor my father and mother." I would then eat dinner, wash the dishes, and then go back to writing until bedtime. On Saturdays, I did chores and then wrote page after page of, "I will honor my father and mother." Sundays, I wrote.

I couldn't play outside, watch TV, or have any recreational or free time. I was ten years old and wanted to go outside to play, but I had to write. I'm not exaggerating when I say I must have written that phrase thousands of times. My hand was in such excruciating pain, tears streamed down my face, as I wrote. I couldn't let them see me crying, though, or I would be punished more severely.

"Your parents don't want you."

I didn't complain about the abuse. How could I? My foster parents had no sympathy for the nightmare I was living. They were the source of the cruelty. The main emotion they felt for me was contempt.

I was constantly threatened; and if I dared to question their authority, I was slapped. I grew up feeling like trash, because I was constantly told that's what I

A Rough Beginning

was. "Your own parents don't even want you," they would sneer.

Even though all of the physical abuse came from my foster mother, both foster parents constantly condemned me and told me I was ugly and stupid. I was belittled, bullied, and told in no uncertain terms that I wouldn't amount to anything, because I was too stupid. No matter how hard I tried, I could not meet my foster parents' expectations. I believe I was most damaged, emotionally and physically, in this last foster placement.

Other foster kids would come and go; I was stuck there. I felt inadequate and incompetent. I was slapped around, things were thrown at me, and I would end up with a knot on my head or a bruise on my body. I tried hard to be quiet and not complain. I had no one to talk to. No one would listen to my cries for help. All I wanted was to be loved...

The overwhelming majority of my childhood memories are painful, with one slight exception. The one pleasant memory I have is when my biological mother came to visit me when I was about nine or ten years old. As my mom sat in a chair, I sat at her feet, playing with toys she brought me. I was happy at last. I was finally having a good time, and it felt amazing! My mom and I were laughing, and she told me she loved me.

Of course, my foster mother had to destroy my brief respite of happiness. After my mom left, my foster mother immediately called the welfare department and told them that I did not want to see my mom again and that my biological mother must be kept away from me. That was not true at all! I <u>never</u> said I didn't want to see my mom. I enjoyed my brief time with her, and I wanted to see her again. My time with her had been filled with joy!

I was devastated when the cold realization hit me that I would probably never see my mom again. My foster mother seemed to derive a sick pleasure from hurting me and robbing me of the happiness I derived from my mom's visit. My foster mother cruelly snatched away and crushed to smithereens what little joy I had experienced in my short life.

In addition to destroying any chance of seeing my mom again, my foster mother blocked a relationship I could have had with my half-brother, who was about two years old at the time. When my mom came to visit, that was the one time I was able to see him. I don't know what happened to him. I can't even recall his name. I never saw him or my mom again.

"I begged them…"

I have a biological full brother named Joe, who is one year older than me. During my childhood, he and I were usually placed in separate foster homes. When I was nine, and he was ten, we were blessed to be able to spend about three years together in my last foster home.

A Throwaway Kid

Unfortunately, Joe was slapped around and beat up quite a bit by both our foster parents. He finally reached his breaking point when he was about 13, and he ran away. The welfare department found him, and he was then placed in a different foster home.

Joe later told me that he begged the welfare department to remove me from that house. "I begged them to take you out of there," he said, "but they refused." He told the social worker, "Man, all we do is get hit and beat on." Still, they refused to remove me from that dreadful environment.

Sadly, the welfare department, at that time, didn't give foster parents the same oversight, scrutiny, and supervision they're given today. It's my opinion that the social workers felt that as long as I was fed and had clean clothes, that was sufficient. It didn't matter if foster children were nurtured and given quality care; all that was required was basic care: food, shelter, and clothing.

I saw Joe again when we were in our 30s, and he stayed with me for a couple of years. We lost touch again, and I haven't seen him or talked to him for over 40 years. Although I've tried to locate him, I haven't been able to find him.

The last time I talked to Joe, we talked about spiritual matters. He told me he accepted Jesus as his Savior and Lord. Joe said that he loved Jesus and that he had been baptized in the Holy Spirit. I may not see Joe again in this life, but I know I'll see him in heaven, where we will have a glorious reunion. No one will be able to separate us again!

"Can I go to the tent meeting?"

When I was 13, on my way home one day, I passed a tent revival. I felt an excitement and expectation I hadn't felt before, and I wanted to go inside. Something was tugging at my heart, compelling me to enter the tent. I believe it was the Holy Spirit of God pulling on my heart like metal to a magnet.

A Throwaway Kid

I thank Jesus for that early experience of being drawn to the tent. It's my first recollection of Him personally calling to me. I'll never forget it.

I was excited! I rushed home to get permission to attend the revival, but my hopes were quickly dashed. My foster parents told me to stay away from that tent. They threatened to beat me within an inch of my life if I went inside. You see, we were of a different faith background, and I would be punished by my foster parents if I wandered from our religious denomination.

I was forced to follow the religious status quo and attend the church within our denomination. I didn't understand what was being taught. No one took time to thoroughly explain the Gospel message to me or tell me about the astonishing love of Jesus. Ironically, I couldn't find God in "His House." The "House of God" we attended was devoid of His presence and power.

A Rough Beginning

Our family's religious routine consisted of my foster parents attending early morning church services on Sunday with the older foster children. After service, they all went to breakfast together, while I was forced to walk to a later service. Joe had already run away, so I walked to church alone.

I attended a private religious school for eight years, which added to the trauma of my childhood. Two of the teachers were verbally and physically abusive; therefore, there was a huge disconnect from what they said and what they did. Their cruel behavior was entirely different from what they taught, so I erected an emotional wall and didn't pay attention to what they said in class.

By the time I transferred to public high school, I was a broken teenager at a crossroads. I wanted to be loved desperately, but I was filled with rage. I was not your typical sweet teenage girl.

After a particularly bad browbeating from my foster mother, when I was 14, I contemplated suicide. I was outside walking and thought about stepping in front of a car. At the last minute, I came to my senses and changed my mind. Right then and there, I hardened my heart. No matter what my foster parents did to me, I wasn't going to allow myself to be hurt.

"To hell with them," I thought. "I'll take care of myself. I'm not depending on them to help me anymore. No one will ever hurt me again!"

I became fiercely resolute and determined to survive. Although I didn't have thoughts of suicide after that, it was as though I suddenly had ice coursing through my veins. Even if I saw someone lying injured on the sidewalk, I made up in my mind that I would step over them. I could care less. I didn't need anything or anybody.

By the time I was 16, I had a tremendous contempt for people. In my mind, everyone was cruel, and I trusted no one. Since all I had experienced was cruelty, I didn't know how to initiate and sustain healthy relationships.

Given that I had not been loved and treated with kindness, I didn't know how to love or be kind. Because I wasn't shown gentleness, I didn't know how to be gentle. Patience wasn't extended to me; therefore, I didn't know how to exercise patience with others. All I knew was how to survive and protect myself from being hurt.

"Don't talk to me!"

I hardened my heart on one hand; on the other hand, I still desperately wanted to be loved and to have friends. In an attempt to make friends in high school, I started saying hi every day to one of my classmates. Each day, she refused to acknowledge my greeting.

Finally, one day, she blurted out, "Don't talk to me! Please don't walk beside me." I knew from that day not to bother her, and I stopped trying to make friends.

A Throwaway Kid

My peers treated me with disdain. "She's just a foster kid," they would snicker. The other students thought I was low-life trash, and they weren't shy about telling me so. I was relentlessly ridiculed and mocked.

Though I received no sympathy from my foster families or peers, I now know Jesus cared and was saddened by the abuse I endured. The Bible demonstrates His deep love in John 11:35, declaring, *Jesus wept.*

In John 11:1-44, Jesus' friend Lazarus became sick, died, and was buried. Jesus knew He would ultimately raise His friend from the dead, but that didn't stop Him from having compassion to the point of weeping over what Lazarus and his family had to endure.

Even while I was going through a painful childhood, Jesus loved me and had a plan for me. No amount of hatred from the world could stop Him from loving me and coming to my rescue. To this day, I don't feel anger or animosity toward my abusers. I'm just happy that I have Jesus as my Savior and

A Rough Beginning

Lord. I have forgiven those who hurt me, because I know that Jesus has forgiven me for my sins. Mark 11:25-26 instructs:

> ^{25}*And when ye stand praying, forgive, if ye have ought against any: that your Father also which is in heaven may forgive you your trespasses. ^{26}But if ye do not forgive, neither will your Father which is in heaven forgive your trespasses.*

I am compelled by God's love to forgive, because God has mercifully forgiven me for every sin I have committed or will commit. Romans 5:8 reminds me:

> *But God commendeth his love toward us, in that, while we were yet sinners, Christ died for us.*

The love of God has set me gloriously free from the painful memories of my past. Because of the remarkable life God has given me, I am driven to share my story with others. I want everyone to know there is love, peace, and joy available through the power of Christ and His salvation!

There is freedom from darkness through Jesus Christ! He liberates the lost, hopeless, and abandoned. He rescues them out of darkness and places them in His marvelous light. Always turn to Him and trust Him for deliverance. No matter what you face, He is your answer. He is your deliverer!

> *35Who shall separate us from the love of Christ? shall tribulation, or distress, or persecution, or famine, or nakedness, or peril, or sword? ... 38For I am persuaded, that neither death, nor life, nor angels, nor principalities, nor powers, nor things present, nor things to come, 39Nor height, nor depth, nor any other creature, shall be able to separate us from the love of God, which is in Christ Jesus our Lord. (Romans 8:35, 38-39)*

Chapter Two
Time to Grow Up

I could no longer stand being abused at school and at home. I finally dropped out of school and left my foster home. I survived by doing odd jobs, cleaning houses, and working in restaurant kitchens.

I was all alone now. I basically hung out on the streets looking for love, but not finding it. Every now and then, someone was kind enough to take me in and get me off the streets, temporarily. I had no lasting friendships nor serious relationships. Boys would only use and abuse me.

When I think back on this period of my life, it amazes me that with all the stress and heartbreak I experienced, I didn't rely on drugs or alcohol for "relief." I did, however, occasionally drink a beer. I thank God that I didn't have a desire for hard liquor or drugs and that my life was not further complicated by substance abuse.

"Starting over…"

When I was about 18, I moved to a small seaside town in Ohio. I rented a room from a nice couple, and we became friends. I was finally with people who truly seemed to care about me. They didn't ridicule or belittle me; on the contrary, we laughed and had good times together.

While out with friends one evening, I met a handsome man named Mitch. We were immediately attracted to one another and began dating. Over time, as we grew closer, we began an intimate relationship, which resulted in me getting pregnant at 21 years of age.

Mitch and I wanted to do what was right, so we married in a civil ceremony. I was grateful that he married me. I had been told

Time to Grow Up

most of my life that I was ugly and worthless. I was told countless times I would never amount to anything. Now I had someone to love me. I was thankful Mitch was willing to unite his life with mine in marriage.

After Mitch's dad passed away, we moved into his dad's house and assumed the mortgage payments. We were blessed to have a home of our own near a lovely park by the sea.

Many women would have given anything to have my life. On the outside, I appeared to lead an idyllic existence heard about in fairytales. Mitch and I were a young married couple with a baby on the way, and we lived in a perfect location.

It wasn't long after we married, though, that Mitch and I began experiencing problems in our marriage. Almost immediately, Mitch began living as if he were a bachelor, and he drank heavily. He refused to take me anywhere, not even to buy groceries. I had to walk to the grocery store and bring the groceries home in a shopping cart.

Even so, I didn't complain. How could I? Mitch had taken a chance on this ugly, worthless woman. I accepted my life and thought to myself, "I should be thankful."

"Can't you do anything right?"

Our quarrels escalated to physical violence. If things weren't done to Mitch's liking, he slapped me around. Before long, the slaps intensified to brutal punches. I had no one to confide in and felt isolated. My dream life quickly deteriorated into a nightmarish hell on earth.

Fear and insecurity invaded my life once again, brought on by Mitch's heavy drinking and drunken rages. I didn't know where to turn. With a baby on the way, I felt that I had no escape. I didn't want my child to experience the same sense of abandonment I had.

I was determined to make my marriage work for the sake of our child. I longed for the family I never had, and I resolved to stick it out. Maybe if I worked really hard, I could provide my child with the life I had been denied when I was young.

Nonetheless, I felt trapped in a vicious cycle of abuse. When Mitch wasn't violent, I was filled with hope that things would get better. Then he would beat me, and hope would once again be lost. Between the emotional, hormonal ups and downs of my pregnancy and the unnerving upheaval of spousal abuse, I was a complete wreck.

I didn't complain to anyone, and I soon learned the art of covering up my bruises with makeup. Though our marriage was spiraling out of control, I didn't actually expect anything better. After all, I'd been conditioned to believe I was unworthy and undeserving of anything good. I had been abused all my life, and this was a familiar environment.

Through my childhood experiences, I had been trained not to complain. It was all my fault, and I wasn't worthy enough to receive nice things.

As a result of my upbringing, I was suspicious and uneasy when things seemed to go well. I didn't trust anyone who wanted to treat me with respect, dignity, or compassion.

I had been thoroughly desensitized to normal human emotion. I didn't know how to expect or demand the best for myself. The deviant standard routine for me was getting up in the morning, brushing my teeth, and getting slapped.

"This is what I deserve."

In spite of being married, I was lonely. Though I wanted my husband's love desperately, it was always out of reach. I kept wondering, "What's wrong with me?" Other people seemed happy. The problem had to be me. That's what I'd always been told, and that lie tormented me.

"There's something wrong with you."

"You're not worthy to be loved."

When Mitch kicked me with steel toe boots with all his might, I figured it was somehow my fault. I must have provoked him in some way. I received a hairline fracture that bothers me to this day.

There was a bright spot in our marriage: the birth of our son, John. My life changed in an instant. I finally experienced true love when I first held him in my arms. Here was someone who was eager to receive my love and who loved me unconditionally. I poured out every ounce of love I had on this sweet baby boy. I knew my purpose was to take care of my child. I was going to be sure to provide him with the love, comfort, nurture, and protection I had not received.

I don't recollect Mitch ever telling me he loved me. He was extremely hateful, and I don't think he was capable of loving. The reason we married wasn't because we loved each other. We married because I got pregnant. In my mind, this horrible marriage was my punishment, and it was what I deserved.

A Throwaway Kid

Mitch wasted a lot of money on alcohol and bar-hopping; consequently, I wasn't allowed to buy anything to decorate the house. All we had were plastic curtains on the windows. Although we lived in a beautiful location, the house we lived in was in desperate need of repairs and renovation.

Mitch's brother lived with us for several months. Mitch was indescribably cruel to him, and he eventually moved out. In addition, he couldn't stomach the way Mitch beat me. His brother felt helpless to stop Mitch's violence. There were no advocates for victims of spousal abuse at that time; it was something that was accepted.

The dysfunctionality of our home intensified. One particularly disturbing incident that stands out in my mind is an evening when I made dinner, and Mitch didn't like the taste of what I'd cooked. He threw me on the floor and smashed the food in my face so forcefully that I almost choked to death.

Memories came flooding in, flashbacks of when someone else made me choke when

I was very young, as they forced food in my mouth. I saw myself in that driveway again, playing with sticks and leaves, when I wasn't deemed worthy enough to play with real toys.

I didn't deserve to be happy. I had no value. It was endlessly reinforced in the depths of my soul that I was trash, a throwaway kid.

"Leave my mommy alone!"

I tried to shield our son, John, from the shroud of negativity that constantly enveloped our home. I found a wonderful escape for us down the street at the park and at the beach. John and I thoroughly enjoyed our neighborhood. I frequently took John for strolls around the community and walks to the store. Mitch chose not to join us at the park or go for walks with us, and we didn't go on family outings.

Although the view outside our home was magnificent, when I stepped through the door of our home, it was dark and menacing.

A Throwaway Kid

Mitch was there, ready to unleash a tirade of verbal and physical abuse. Once, while I was holding John in my arms, Mitch came at me and was about to punch me. I quickly shifted John to my other side to keep the blow from hitting him, and I took the brunt of the punch. The one thing on my mind was positioning my body to protect my baby.

I could not possibly know what would trigger Mitch's violent outbursts. It might be something as trivial as not preparing dinner on time, or I didn't buy what he wanted at the grocery store.

As John grew older, it became more of a struggle to hide what was going on. Most of the time, I tried to put on a happy face and act as though nothing were wrong. It was only a matter of time before Mitch erupted uncontrollably in front of him.

Mitch rushed at me, and he started pounding me to the ground. John, at two years old, came to my defense. My little son grabbed a curtain rod and started whacking his dad with it.

"Leave my mommy alone!"

It shocked Mitch so badly that, for a while, he stopped beating me. There was finally a period when things seemed almost normal, and family life resumed, but it wasn't to last for long.

When I became pregnant with our second son, Jim, I had such severe morning sickness, there were times I couldn't get out of bed. The nausea was intense, and my doctor seriously contemplated hospitalizing me. Mitch was not sympathetic at all. If I didn't get out of bed on time to make his breakfast, he beat me.

"I'm going to kill you."

One night Mitch called me from a bar. He had been drinking heavily and was angry and delusional. He told me that when he got home, he was going to kill me. When he made that threat, I took him seriously. He was a cruel man, and I didn't doubt what he said. I wasn't about to wait around for him to come home. After two and a half years of enduring a marriage from hell, I gathered up John and what few clothes I could, and we left.

Friends took me in temporarily, while I tried to figure out what to do. After Jim was born, I was blessed to find a job, and I moved to my own apartment. I divorced Mitch, but he continued to visit me and the children (usually when he was drunk after bar-hopping, and the bars had closed).

It was extraordinarily difficult being a single mother; nevertheless, I was determined to give my babies the best care that I could. When there wasn't enough food, I skipped meals. Things were tight financially, and I could only afford to eat every other day. No matter how tight things were, though, I made sure my kids ate every day.

The struggle of being a single mother was compounded by my involvement in a serious car accident; I was hospitalized for 30 days. I still experience adverse effects from the accident and suffer with recurrent back pain.

"The end of the world is here!"

Right before the car accident, Mitch had a complete mental breakdown and began hearing voices. After he left a bar one night, he came to visit me and the kids. He was drunk and began mumbling incoherently and irrationally. Nothing he said was making sense. All of a sudden, he began running around my apartment, screaming over and over, "It's the end of the world!" I was frightened by his erratic behavior, and I called the police. They transported him to Toledo State Hospital, an asylum for the insane.

Mitch was diagnosed with paranoid schizophrenia, and he was hospitalized for approximately one month. When he was released, he seemed to be doing much better. Mitch and I agreed to try to work things out, for the sake of our family. We didn't want our children to become the casualties of a broken home. The kids and I moved back into the family home with Mitch.

"Things seemed better..."

Mitch received counseling and stopped drinking. When the kids and I moved back home, he never laid a hand on me again. He wasn't even verbally abusive. He was a different man, and he was much kinder; however, I still wouldn't call our relationship a loving one. Our relationship was more like friends who had a shared mission of providing a home for our kids.

Although the atmosphere of negativity and violence was gone from our home, John and Jim still didn't have a warm or close relationship with their dad. He didn't abuse them; he chose to ignore them. I thank God the kids have no memory of their dad's abuse toward me and no memory that he was not active in their lives. They were too young to remember that brief period. John was three at this point, and Jim was a baby.

Mitch continued seeing a psychiatrist after his release from the state hospital. The psychiatrist prescribed medication for psychosis and schizophrenia, which seemed to cause undesirable emotional side effects. The doctor kept increasing the dosage, trying to bring Mitch relief. I personally believe the dosage was too high.

About three months after I moved back home, I was standing in our downstairs bedroom and heard a loud bang! I rushed out of the bedroom and into the living room to see what happened. (Our bedroom and living room were separated by a thin wall.)

Mitch had calmly walked into the living room, sat down, and shot himself with a double-barreled shotgun he had retrieved from a bedroom. I was devastated! Mitch's suicide took me completely by surprise. There were no warning signs to indicate that he was even remotely thinking about taking his own life.

I thank God that I have no memory of what Mitch looked like after he shot himself. (I believe it is God's protection.) I rushed to a neighbor's house to get help, and the police came immediately. They went upstairs to get the kids; and as they exited the house with John and Jim, the officers made sure the kids did not see their dad's body.

"Where are you?"

I felt lost, as I stood outside muttering, as if speaking to Mitch, "Where are you? What's going on?" I was extremely depressed and blackness enveloped me like a heavy, thick veil. I don't mean just darkness; I mean total blackness. Blackness seemed to be everywhere. Just when my life was getting back on track, I was plunged into the pit again. Yet, God had a better plan for me...

> *6For God, who commanded the light to shine out of darkness, hath shined in our hearts... 8We are troubled on every side, yet not distressed; we are perplexed, but not in despair; 9Persecuted, but not forsaken; cast down, but not destroyed; (2 Corinthians 4:6a, 8-9)*

Part Two

Chapter Three
Trust God

The road to recovery after Mitch's death was rocky and filled with emotional pitfalls. I was reeling from the shock of his suicide. To say that I was a basket case is an understatement. Though most of our life together had been chaotic and violent, we had begun a new chapter.

We were headed for restoration, and I was filled with hope for a new beginning for our family. I don't know why he ended his life. He was psychotic and schizophrenic, which I'm sure must have contributed to his fateful decision that night.

The children and I lived in the family home for a brief time after Mitch's death, but the memories of the suicide weighed heavily on us. A doctor recommended that we move out of the house.

I was a single mother, again, and things were rough for a while. It was hard to accomplish even mundane daily chores. A friend, Tom, stepped in to help out when he could. If I needed to run errands or go grocery shopping, he was there to help me and the kids. Over time, our friendship grew, and we fell in love and got married.

"It's going to be fine; I'm here."

When I married Tom, the acute anxiety I suffered from my first marriage still lingered. I often cried at night, and I'd wake up from nightmares, screaming, wanting to run away and flee to safety. Tom would hold me and say, "It's going to be fine; I'm here. You don't have to worry; I'm here."

It took a year for me to go to bed without being fully dressed in street clothes. I suffered from posttraumatic stress. I was constantly in fight or flight mode, that basic instinct to attack or flee when posed with a threat, even though the dangers of my past were only in my mind.

Tom was patient with me and put up with my unpredictable behavior. My anxiety was so severe, there were times Tom had to take me to the hospital, where I was given injections to calm my nerves. Tom did not give up on me. He kept praying for me, and the Lord miraculously delivered me from all anxiety.

If it wasn't for Tom, I don't know what I would've done. I know the Lord sent him to me. When I was hurting, Tom held me and helped me through those rough times. Unlike most other people in my life, he didn't threaten me or beat me. He just loved me.

"Honey, what's wrong?"

When I reached retirement age, in order to get my pension, I had to order a copy of my birth certificate. When I received it and saw what was on it, I started crying uncontrollably. Tom was sitting in a chair in the kitchen, and I knelt beside him, crying into his lap. He asked me, "Honey, what's wrong?" I replied through my sobs, "I have no first name on my birth certificate." He lovingly responded, "You can have my name." I said, "Honey, I don't want people to call me Neff Neff."

We both burst out laughing. Tom had a way of turning things around. He could turn a sad moment into a glad one. He took me out of the depths of sorrow and helped me put things in perspective. I legally added my name, Kathy, to my birth certificate, and the crisis passed.

"The greatest love…"

The greatest relationship I've ever had or will ever have is with the Lord Jesus Christ. Tom nor I were following Jesus when we first met. Neither of us understood that we could have an intimate relationship with God.

It was Tom who first committed to a relationship with God through Jesus Christ. It was his strong desire to draw nearer to the Lord that compelled me to draw nearer to God, also.

Once we started attending church, I performed the typical religious duties like paying tithes. I showed up for church services on Sunday, but I rarely thought about God the other six days of the week. I had a casual relationship with Him, not an intimate one.

I loved Jesus, but I wasn't completely surrendered to Him. Even so, I enjoyed the times I spent in church. I especially loved praising and worshiping God. I loved learning about Him, and I enjoyed meeting new people.

I loved the Lord, but there were times I stumbled. I was not and still am not perfect. If I were perfect, I wouldn't need a Savior. People sometimes get a false impression of God, because Christians stumble and make mistakes. They fail to understand Christians are simply imperfect people who worship and follow a perfect God.

A Throwaway Kid

Each time I stumble, God helps me move forward. I never fall back; I fall forward into His loving arms, and He lifts me right back up. God uses every experience – the good, the bad, and the ugly – to teach us and help us mature.

One of the ways God helps us to grow and mature is through the power of His Holy Spirit. When I received the baptism in the Holy Spirit years ago, it was powerful! It happened in a service where I was called up to the front of the church to receive a prophecy.

I walked up there with my hands tightly folded. I had seen people "fall out in the spirit" before, and I was having no part of it. I made up my mind. "Man, I ain't falling on no floor and getting slain in no spirit. I'm keeping my hands together."

Then the prophecy came forth: "The Lord says you need more joy in your life." The next thing I knew, my hands flew apart and down I went!

Prior to that, my mindset was, "Why should I smile? I'm not worth anything. I have no value. What right do I have to be happy?" The Lord broke that hard, calloused shell that night. He baptized me in His Spirit and filled me with His joy.

I love attending church. I have a sense of expectancy that something incredible is going to happen when the saints of God gather together. It's exciting to hear each new revelation God gives my pastor to share with the congregation, as he pours through the Scriptures. I'm very thankful for the support of my pastor and church family.

When I go to church, I expect a divine encounter with God, as I worship and praise Him. I must admit that I don't socialize with the congregation as much as I should. The Lord is working on me about interacting more with my church family. It's a work in progress, and I am improving.

Because of the cruelty and violence I suffered in my past, it's hard to draw close to people and develop relationships. My attitude in the past was, "I don't need you; I can take care of myself." Of course, that attitude is being dealt with by the Lord, and He is helping me mature spiritually and emotionally.

"A unique sense of humor…"

I have somewhat of a reputation for my unique sense of humor. On one occasion, a group of ladies gathered at my house to learn to make pie crust. Joann was an excellent baker, and she was giving us baking tips. While she was teaching, I got a little bored. So, I took a pinch of dough and flung it, and it landed in one of the ladies' ears. Needless to say, the ladies put me in timeout.

On another occasion, we went to Becky's house to bake bread. By the time we finished, I had dough all over her kitchen. I think it took her almost a month to clean up the mess. For some reason, she hasn't invited me over to bake, again. Each time I ask

Trust God

her, "Becky, do you want me to come over and bake bread?" she quickly says, "No!"

I host a Bible study group in my home on Thursday evenings. It's a treasured time of praise and worship, fellowship, and studying the Word of God. Of course, I have to lighten it up a little at times by injecting my unique sense of humor. There are two friends that especially get me going: Greta and Rita. We love to laugh!

I evoke a party atmosphere wherever I go. My motto is, "You've got to learn to laugh." I try to draw laughter out of people, and it began when I received the prophecy, "The Lord said you need more joy in your life." On that night, He infused me with joy that's been overflowing full force ever since.

No one can take this joy away. It's not a product of circumstances, or surroundings, or people. He infused me with His joy, and I've learned to laugh. He's placed deep within me a fountain perpetually bubbling over with joy. It's become who I am. If anyone doesn't like it, they can complain to the

A Throwaway Kid

Lord, because He's the one who gave me a new life!

My son, Jim, reminded me just how unique my sense of humor can be at times. He asked me, "Mom, do remember what you pulled at work when they were closing down the company?" "No," I said innocently. "What did I do?" My son was all too eager to jog my memory.

The company I worked for was transferring overseas. My boss came in and sternly announced, "I want everything in this tool shed packed and shipped to headquarters!" So, after we packed up everything, I swept up all the dirt from the floor, gathered all the garbage, even grabbed someone's leftover sandwich, packed it all up, and sent it to headquarters!

They could not accuse me of being disobedient. I did what I was told. Everything went. When my boss checked back, yelling, "Did you ship everything to headquarters?!" I replied, "I sent everything, boss, I sent everything."

"Tom was my best friend."

Tom and I were exceptionally close. We did a lot of joking and laughing, and we truly loved being together. I believe one of the reasons my marriage to Tom was blessed was because we became good friends first before we started a romantic relationship.

Our romance grew from our friendship. With the underpinning of love, we were able to build our family on a sure foundation that could not be shaken when spiritual, emotional, and physical storms hit.

We were a perfect match. Tom also had a unique sense of humor. He usually only expressed it between us and wouldn't normally let it show around other people. One day, Tom told me I could go shopping at a local clothing store.

He said, "Here's the credit card. Get anything you want."

Man, I was ready by 9:00 a.m. I arrived at the store, only to find out it was closed for two weeks due to renovations. I came home and said disappointingly, "They're closed for two weeks for remodeling." Tom gave me a sly grin and said, "Yeah, I know."

I had my revenge, though. I went to a friend's house to bake homemade bread. When I got home, after I took the bread into the house, I wrapped up a brick and put it in the car. Tom knew I was baking bread that day, and he was excited about having homemade bread with dinner.

When he came home from work, I said, "Honey, will you bring in the bread?" He brought that heavy bag in and didn't say a word.

I said, "Well, do you want me to slice you a piece now?" He replied, "No, no, I'm not hungry." I finally opened it up and showed him that it was a brick, and we both had a good laugh.

One weekend, Tom was building a clubhouse for the boys, and I wanted to help him out. I picked up a large board, intending to hand it to him. As I picked up the board, I swung it around and hit him in the back of the head. I quickly apologized. "Oh, honey, I'm so sorry." I turned around again and hit him in the front of the head. I sheepishly asked, "Honey, does this mean I'm fired?"

He chose his words carefully as he answered slowly, "I don't remember hiring you." I immediately responded, "I'll go in the house and make you something to eat."

"Thank you for answering my prayer."

Tom was passionate about helping people. On one of his missions of mercy, he drove someone to Toledo, about an hour away from our home, and the car broke down. When Tom called to tell me about the car, I threw a fit.

After we hung up, I was standing in the kitchen, looking out the window. I declared to God, "You're a great God, and Tom's doing a good thing, and now we don't have a car."

All of a sudden, I felt God's presence. The anger that I'd felt about the car a moment earlier melted like wax in the warm embrace of God's love. Basking in His embrace, I didn't care anything about the car. All I cared about was remaining in His presence.

Tom got the car fixed and came home. When he walked through the door, I could tell he was a little leery, since I had thrown such a fit. I have to be honest. I had been a real jerk on the phone.

When he came through the door, I was still enjoying God's embrace and had a big smile on my face. Tom looked at me and then exclaimed, "Thank you, Jesus, for answering my prayer!"

Apparently, Tom had been praying, "Change my wife's attitude," at the same time I was at home praying. We were standing together as one, in agreement, in prayer, without knowing it. God heard us and answered our prayers.

Tom taught me a lot about blessing others, and I remember it to this day. We had several boys stay with us intermittently,

Trust God

who had nowhere to live. More than physical shelter, they needed to know they were loved.

I drew on my own experience as a child. I know first-hand that children need more than a roof over their heads, clothes on their backs, and food in their bellies. They need encouragement, nurturing, and to know that someone loves them. They must also be told that God loves them. It's imperative to share the love of Jesus.

I am blessed by God, and I love to bless others. God's blessings are so rich in my life that they overflow. He not only gives me an excess of physical blessings like food and clothing, He produces a flood of spiritual blessings, such as joy, peace, and love. The Lord gives far above what I can imagine.

Now unto him that is able to do exceeding abundantly above all that we ask or think, according to the power that worketh in us... (Ephesians 3:20)

"As for me and my house..."

...choose you this day whom ye will serve...but as for me and my house, we will serve the LORD. (Joshua 24:15)

As Tom and I grew together in the Lord, it strengthened our family. The perfect framework for families is found in God's Word:

21Submitting yourselves one to another in the fear of God. 22Wives, submit yourselves unto your own husbands, as unto the Lord. 23For the husband is the head of the wife, even as Christ is the head of the church: and he is the saviour of the body. 24Therefore as the church is subject unto Christ, so let the wives be to their own husbands in every thing. 25Husbands, love your wives, even as Christ also loved the church, and gave himself for it; 26That he might sanctify and cleanse it with the washing of water by the word, 27That he might present it to himself a glorious church, not having spot, or wrinkle, or any such thing; but that it should be holy and without blemish. 28So ought men to love their wives as their own bodies. He that loveth his wife loveth himself. 29For no man ever yet hated his own flesh; but nourisheth and cherisheth it, even as the Lord the church: 30For we are members of his body, of his flesh, and of his bones. 31For this cause shall a man leave his father and mother, and shall be joined unto his wife, and they two shall be one flesh. 32This is a great mystery: but I speak concerning Christ and the church. 33Nevertheless let every one of you in particular so love his wife even as himself; and the wife see that she reverence her husband. (Ephesians 5:21-33)

A Throwaway Kid

Some wives read, *Wives submit yourselves unto your own husbands*, and bristle at the thought of having to submit. By reading the passage in context, I believe you will see this is God's perfect plan for marriage.

Verse 21 instructs the husband and wife to submit themselves under each other's authority out of respect for Christ.

Verse 22 instructs the wife to place herself under her husband's authority, as she has placed herself under the Lord's authority. If a woman is not submitted to God's authority, she cannot submit to her husband's authority. When a woman submits to Christ's authority <u>before</u> marriage, she will wait on God's choice, marry the right man for the right reasons, and have no objection submitting to his authority.

Tom and I had this type of marriage. He didn't lord over me and dictate what he wanted me to do. We were submitted to one another in love, and our family was rooted in that love.

Trust God

I had no problem at all recognizing Tom as the head of our household, because he did not rule as an authoritarian seeking his own good. He was a man of God, and he served us, as his family, protected us, and amply provided for us. Tom was sent by God, and I recognized that and embraced it.

Verses 23-24 explain that the husband is the head of the wife as Christ is the head of the church. When a woman marries a godly man, he is submitted to Christ and treats her with love and respect.

Verses 25-33 describe the relationship the husband is to have with his wife. He is to love her just as passionately as Christ loves His Bride, the church.

Verse 29 emphasizes that Christ cherishes and nurtures His Bride. That is the example He set for husbands.

Tom loved me with that type of love; therefore, our marriage produced the fruit of God's love. The Word of God declares that a husband should protect his wife, provide for her, love and encourage her, and give his life for her as Christ gave His life for His Bride.

God's Word goes on to explain that a husband must love his wife as he loves his own body, because a man who loves his wife loves himself. No man ever hated his own body. He feeds and takes care of it. The husband and wife become one, as the body of Christ is one.

The closing verse (verse 33) directs a husband to love his wife as he loves himself, and the wife must respect her husband.

This is God's plan for marriage. It's not hard for a husband and wife to follow God's plan when both are submitted to Him. This is the type of marriage I was blessed by God to have with Tom. God is all-knowing and all-powerful. We must trust Him and do things His way. He knows what He's doing, and He's much smarter than we are.

In Ephesians 6, God goes further and lays out his plan for children within the family.

Trust God

¹Children, obey your parents in the Lord: for this is right. ²Honour thy father and mother; which is the first commandment with promise; ³That it may be well with thee, and thou mayest live long on the earth. ⁴And, ye fathers, provoke not your children to wrath: but bring them up in the nurture and admonition of the Lord. (Ephesians 6:1-4)

Children should obey their parents, because the Bible says it's the right thing to do. When children honor their father and mother, God promises that all will go well, and they will have a long life on earth.

Unlike the perversion of this Scripture that my foster mother portrayed, this passage instructs fathers to be careful not to make their children bitter about life. They are to bring their children up in godly discipline and instruction.

Tom lived these Bible verses every day. John and Jim adored Tom. They didn't see him as their stepfather; they thought of him as their father. He loved the kids, and they loved him.

"Our foundation was God."

When a family is built on the foundation of God's love, they will be solid as a rock. God's plan for the family is one that can be trusted, especially in bad times. When things are difficult, the family who follows Him will overcome adversities together, since they've put God in control.

> *For I know the thoughts that I think toward you, saith the LORD, thoughts of peace, and not of evil, to give you an expected end. (Jeremiah 29:11)*

Because Tom and I trusted God, we knew that His plan for our family was good; therefore, His plan gave us hope to receive His blessings every day of our lives. God's plan for our family was not to harm us. His plan was to prosper us: spirit, soul, and body. His

Trust God

plan is to defeat evil through overwhelming victory in Christ Jesus our Lord!

Tom and I lived each day saturated in the marvelous blessings of God. We did everything as a family. We went to the zoo, local fairs, tourist attractions, and went on vacations together. We were baptized as a family when the boys were 8 and 10. My kids are now grown and on their own, and we're still a close-knit family.

Many times, after a hard day's work, Tom would gather the boys up and take them to the park and beach across the street, while I prepared dinner. He'd put them on the merry-go-round and spin them around, and they'd squeal with joy! Tom loved John and Jim, and he loved spending time with them. God blessed us to live in a spectacular location to raise a family, and we took advantage of it whenever we could.

I wanted my sons to have everything I didn't have when I was a child. I wanted them to know how much they were loved. I didn't deprive them of anything. On the contrary, I might have given them a little too much. I suppose I was trying to live my childhood through them. I wanted them to have the childhood I never had.

When the kids were young, sometimes I'd let the dishes sit during the day, while we played "hide and seek" or "pick-up sticks." When they went to bed, then I did the dishes. I thoroughly enjoyed my kids. I tried to give them love, a sense of belonging, and security. They knew without a doubt that they were loved.

Before I had children, my love had been rejected many times; no one wanted to love me. When I had my sons, I was able to take all that locked-up love and pour it out on them. In return, they have given me an immeasurable amount of love and joy. God has truly blessed me!

My youngest son, Jim, called me one day and said, "Mom, I never said thank you." "Thank you for what?" I asked. He replied, "For giving me such a good childhood." As a parent, that's one of the best compliments you can receive from your child.

Tom and I spent quality time with the kids and demonstrated to them that we were a family who loved each other. We didn't show love by merely saying the words, "I love you." We proved it by our actions.

Train up a child in the way he should go: and when he is old, he will not depart from it. (Proverbs 22:6)

"The adventures of John & Jim..."

Tom and I made every effort to give our sons a solid Christian upbringing. There were moments, however, when John and Jim pushed our patience to its limit and stepped on our very last nerve. At the time, those moments were not particularly pleasant. In hindsight, those were some of the funniest, most endearing and memorable moments of our family life together.

Following is just a taste of some of the childhood antics of John and Jim. I hope they put a smile on your face.

When John was about five, I had to spank him. With all the love I could muster, I gently said, "John, the only reason I spanked you is because I love you." In typical John fashion, he replied, "Why do you have to love me so much?"

When John was eight years old, he whacked Jim with a rock, and Jim started bleeding. At the sight of blood, I panicked and started screaming for Tom! We took Jim to the hospital and got him stitched up. When we got home, I immediately approached John. I said, "John, I want to talk to you." John said, "I knew it, I knew it. I threw a rock, Jim runs into it, and you blame me."

Trust God

❧❧❧❧❧❧❧

One Saturday, John wanted me to get up early. I wasn't quite ready to get up. It was the weekend, and I wanted to sleep in a teeny bit later than usual. That little stinker threw his snapping turtle in bed with me. I leapt out of bed, screaming, "Okay, I'm up!"

❧❧❧❧❧❧❧

John liked to help his dad out with projects around the house and got the bright idea to redo our kitchen floor. In his young six-year-old mind, he thought it would be good to paint the indoor-outdoor carpeting we had recently installed. To add insult to injury, the carpet hadn't been down for even 24 hours!

❧❧❧❧❧❧❧

When John was nine, he gave our curtains "a haircut." We had to buy curtains for the entire house. He had cut every single one of them!

When Jim was a toddler, I took him to a restaurant as a treat. I ordered him one of his favorites: a plate of French fries. When he finished eating, he turned around and put the plate on the head of the man sitting behind us, who was a complete stranger! I grabbed Jim, paid the bill, and left that restaurant in a hurry!

When Jim was four, I took him to the doctor. As we were sitting in the doctor's office, a woman entered in a wheelchair, and she had only one leg. Jim piped up, "Lady, you've got to go back home. You forgot your other leg." I was mortified! The woman, however, thought it was hilarious and burst out laughing.

Trust God

ನಿನಿನಿನಿನಿನಿನಿ

One afternoon, John walked calmly into the house and said nonchalantly, "Jimmy got hit by a car." In the next breath he said, "Hey, we got any pie left?" I said, "What? Are you serious?" "Yeah, and he's laying out there in the street. We got any pie?" I ran out of the house, and I saw Jim's bike under a car down the street. I took off running. Jim was okay and wasn't hurt. I'm so grateful to God that he didn't even have a scratch on him.

ನಿನಿನಿನಿನಿನಿನಿ

If I only had to punish John twice a day, that was an awesome day, and I considered him to be on his best behavior!

ನಿನಿನಿನಿನಿನಿನಿ

We were in church one Sunday, and they passed the collection plate. John got the wrong impression and thought it was money for us to take. He grabbed some of the money! I was trying my best to make him let it go. He had a death grip on it and was not letting go! I was so humiliated.

⁂

One afternoon, the elementary school called me about Jim. He apparently wanted to express his artistic side that day and painted the kid next to him. Inevitably, it soon escalated into a paint war, and many of the kids ended up painted, as well as the teacher. By the time I picked Jim up from school, he was multicolored. I sent a little white boy to school that morning, and I got a multicolored kid back that afternoon.

⁂

As adults, John and Jim are still full of mischief. When they get together, even now, I'm at their mercy. They make me laugh so hard at times, I can't talk. I love my sons so much. Now that they are grown, I pray that the Spirit of God will make them mighty warriors for the Lord!

"Take shelter immediately!"

"A tornado touched down south of Port Clinton and then moved northeast entering the city just west of the intersection of Wilcox Road and Fulton Road. The tornado moved through the heart of the city reaching Lake Erie at Lakeview Park. From there, the tornado moved northeast over Lake Erie to Catawba Island where it finally dissipated after a ten mile long damage path. Four people suffered minor injuries as a result of the tornado. Hardest hit was the Lakeview Park area where two condominiums were blown off their stilts into Lake Erie and many other structures were destroyed. The initial storm damage in Port Clinton occurred along 11th Street where several homes were heavily damaged or destroyed. Significant damage also occurred near 8th and Fulton Streets. As the tornado moved through the city, it damaged the local high school and a hospital. Significant damage also occurred on Catawba Island with several homes damaged and destroyed before the tornado finally

A Throwaway Kid

> dissipated. A total of 24 homes and 16 apartments were destroyed along the damage path with approximately 60 additional homes damaged enough to be deemed uninhabitable. Another 80 structures sustained minor to moderate amounts of damage. The damage path was typically no more than 50 yards in width. Dozens of vehicles were damaged or destroyed by the tornado and hundreds of trees and power poles were toppled."
> (http://www.weather.gov/cle/event_20021002_tornado_outbreak_portclinton)

November 10, 2002, was a beautiful fall day. The weather was perfect. Tom and I went for a walk at Lakeview Park, half a block from our home, and we did fun things around town. After we came home, Tom sat on the couch in the living room, and I went into the kitchen.

I kept hearing tornado warnings. I wasn't worried, though, as I thought to myself, "We don't get tornados." I was standing in front of the refrigerator, which was built into the wall, and then I heard a rumbling in the distance.

Trust God

Tom immediately started praying fervently with everything that was in him. Soon, the refrigerator started bouncing. I thought, "Lord, if I'm coming home, I'm bringing the food!" I tell you, that refrigerator was really bouncing.

I looked toward the back of the house, and part of the roof was gone. Suddenly, I saw hubcaps flying through the air. Tom and I considered taking cover in a bedroom, thought better of it, and decided to stay where we were. I believe the Holy Spirit of God convicted us to stay put: Tom in the living room and me in the kitchen.

If we had gone into that bedroom, we would've been killed. The high winds of the tornado broke the window and stabbed shards of glass into the bed.

I was very afraid, especially when I saw a car sitting in the backyard where our shed used to be. The winds were so violent that my car had a vice embedded in the windshield, a twig from a tree went through my car engine, and a weeping willow crashed onto Tom's El Camino. The tornado annihilated eight houses on our street and in the next block.

Where Tom was sitting, nothing in the living room, not even the pictures on the wall were disturbed. In his den, where all his belongings were, nothing was disrupted. In contrast, everything I owned was destroyed. The whole back of the house was gone.

John and Jim were grown and had moved out of the house by this time. When I told my son, Jim, what happened, he said, "Mom, did you ever think that maybe you should be on your knees more like Dad? None of his stuff got messed up."

Following are pictures of the damage on that fateful day, November 10, 2002. (Source: http://www.weather.gov/cle/event_20021002_tornado_outbreak_portclintonpics)

Trust God

A Throwaway Kid

Trust God

A Throwaway Kid

Trust God

A Throwaway Kid

Following are personal pictures taken before and after the tornado.

Our house before the tornado.

Trust God

Our house after the tornado.

A Throwaway Kid

Tom's El Camino by our house.

Trust God

Our new house.

"An attached bathroom would be nice..."

Months before the tornado hit, I had a desire to have a bathroom attached to our master bedroom. Tom was diabetic, and he had to get up often throughout the night to go to the bathroom. I said, "Lord, it would be nice to have a bathroom right off the bedroom for Tom."

God turned the heartbreak of the tornado into something good. When we built our new house, we designed it with the bathroom connected to our bedroom. God is good!

After the tornado, we were blessed to live with my oldest son, John, for a year, while our new house was being built. John was incredibly thoughtful. He did everything he could for us.

When we went through the tornado, I didn't blame God. I didn't complain or ask, "Why did you let this happen?" I wasn't angry at God when our house was destroyed.

The best lesson I learned from that experience was how unimportant material things are. They can be replaced. You can always get another couch, another table, another washing machine. I learned that even though life is fragile, we are in God's tender care.

"Who are you?"

Our faith would be tested again when Tom's health began to fail. During the last three years of his life, Tom suffered many illnesses; even so, his faith did not falter. As a matter of fact, Tom's faith skyrocketed. Through colon cancer, kidney cancer, heart problems, diabetes, Parkinson's disease, and Alzheimer's, I watched Tom's faith deepen. He read and studied the Word of God every day.

Tom prayed faith-filled prayers, not religious, repetitious, rote prayers out of habit. Tom had an excellent prayer life. It didn't matter if he saw an immediate answer to his prayers or not; Tom trusted God completely to answer in His way and in His time.

Tom loved to worship and praise God with all his heart, soul, mind, and strength. When I played Christian music, I'd see him lifting his hands to the Lord and praising Him. His relationship with God was genuine and could not be shaken, even when his health grew worse. He knew where he was going when his life was over on this earth, and he cherished the thought of living with his King forever!

At the onset of Alzheimer's, I noticed Tom was becoming increasingly forgetful. He usually paid the bills and managed all of our finances; however, we started receiving bills with "Past Due" stamped on them. At that point, I took control of our finances. I realized Tom was no longer capable of managing the household budget.

After Tom retired, as the effects of Alzheimer's intensified, one weekday morning he was a little confused and thought he had to go to work.

Trust God

As he was putting on his shoes, I asked, "Honey, where are you going?" He replied, "I'm going to work."

Thinking quickly, I asked, "Did you forget it's Saturday? You don't have to work today." "Oh, yeah, I forgot," he responded. "I think I'll go back to bed." He then climbed back in bed and fell asleep.

To protect Tom and keep him from wandering off, I had to keep the doors locked. It became apparent that was necessary after he disappeared one evening. I searched and searched, and I couldn't find him.

I called the police, and they located him through a GPS tracking system specifically designed for people who are prone to wander, such as those with Alzheimer's or autism. They found Tom by the railroad tracks two blocks from our home. He was standing there, obviously confused. He didn't know how to get home.

Tom was bedridden the last year of his life. The Alzheimer's disease had been progressively getting worse over a period of three years. During the last year, sometimes he knew me, and sometimes he didn't. On one occasion, Tom looked at me and said, "Who are you?" Without missing a beat, I said, "Marilyn Monroe." Even now, I can see him standing there, staring back at me, asking, "No, really, who are you?" I thought, "Well, your Alzheimer's isn't that bad."

Tom was hospitalized many times and underwent multiple surgeries and lengthy cancer treatments. For over a year, I took complete care of Tom. I was responsible for checking his blood sugar, making sure his medications were filled, making sure he took them properly, and making sure he ate right.

I went from being pampered and having almost no weighty responsibility, to having total responsibility for running the house and taking care of Tom. That was my choice. I loved my husband deeply and did not resent one moment of it. I never said, "I wish I had time for myself." He was the love of my life, and I wanted to take good care of him. I thank God for equipping me in every way to be able to keep Tom out of a nursing home, even in the toughest times.

Tom was an amazing man. He was good to me, and I know that he loved me. He had compassion and was there to hug me and say, "It'll be all right." Tom loved our family, prayed for us, and stuck by us. The least I could do was stick by him when he needed help. In his time of desperate need, Tom was able to reap the bountiful love he had sown into our family over the years.

"It's time for Tom's reward."

I was crying one night, because I didn't want my husband to die. The Lord clearly spoke to me and said, "It's time for Tom's reward." After He said that, I could accept Tom's inevitable passing. I didn't feel led after that to pray that Tom be kept alive. I wanted him to have his reward.

This gracious message from the Lord was His way of warning me that Tom would be passing soon. It was about two months

A Throwaway Kid

later that I would have to draw on that gentle message from God.

On December 19, 2013, the hospice nurse told me that Tom probably would not make it through the night. So, I called the family together, and they came to be by Tom's side: John and Darla; John Jr. and Denise; and Steven and Brittany.

My son, John, laid down on the floor of the living room at 2:30 in the morning, a couple of feet from the bedroom where his dad was sleeping, to get a few minutes of sleep himself. Right after he laid down, I let out a blood-curdling scream! I think John made the leap into the bedroom in one step. At 2:33 a.m., December 20, 2013, Tom, my best friend and the love of my life, passed away. We had been together for 45 years.

A couple of days after Tom died, I was sitting on the bed staring at a blank television screen. I was sobbing and crying, and I was hurting. I cried out to Jesus, "If I only knew if Tom was happy…" I knew where

Trust God

Tom was; I just wanted proof that he was happy.

It reminds me of the centurion and Jairus in the Bible. (Luke 7:1-10; Luke 8:41-42, 49-56) The centurion had such extraordinary faith in Jesus' ability to heal his servant, that he essentially told Jesus, "You don't have to come to my house to heal my servant. Just say the word, and I know he'll be healed." Jairus, on the other hand, wanted Jesus to come to his house to touch his daughter and heal her. In both cases, they had faith. I wonder, though, who had the greater faith?

I had faith, and I knew Tom was in heaven; I just wanted proof that he was happy. The Lord then showed me a vision of Tom. I didn't see anybody else. I saw Tom standing in a white garment with clouds surrounding him. I saw his face, and he didn't have a beard. He looked serene. He seemed to be taking in all of what he was seeing.

Immediately after the Lord showed me the vision, He said to me, "Kathy, where is your faith?" Point taken, Lord. I haven't wavered since.

As I was later contemplating the vision and what the Lord had shown me, I realized Tom didn't have a beard in the vision. At the time of his death, Tom had been sporting a beard for over 40 years. When he was in his 30s, though, he shaved consistently and didn't have a beard. Speaking of when Jesus began His ministry, Luke 3:23 states:

And Jesus himself began to be about thirty years of age...

Jesus was in His prime when He began his ministry, was put on trial, crucified, buried, and raised to life again. 1 John 3:2 says that when we see Jesus, we will be like Him. I believe we will forever be as if we are in the prime of our lives, when we are living in the light of eternity with our King!

"I began to fully trust God."

When I first started attending church with Tom, I felt comfortable. I listened intently, because I wanted to learn; however, I wasn't 100% committed to Jesus. I didn't place 100% confidence in Him. After Tom went on to his reward, my faith deepened. I now give God 100%.

When Tom became seriously ill, he continually prayed, "Lord, take care of my wife." Even when he knew he lay dying, his sole concern was me. My deeper walk with the Lord is the fruit of Tom's prayers.

I now have a more intimate relationship with Jesus. His overwhelming love compels me to praise and worship Him. I have surrendered fully to Him and long for His will to be done and not my own. I know I can fully trust Him. He has been faithful through every trial, even when I didn't realize He was right there walking me through every dark valley.

A Throwaway Kid

Although I had a rough beginning in life, I now know that Jesus was beckoning to me from the start, bidding me to follow Him. As I gave up my agenda and accepted His plan, I began to experience an intimate relationship with the Creator of the universe.

I love studying the Scriptures. I kiss His Word every day and thank Him for it. The more I read His Word, the more intimately I know Him, not merely about Him. When I was a new believer in Christ, I could sense His presence when I was in church; then I'd go home and somehow leave Jesus in the church building. I was "good." I didn't commit adultery, steal, or lie. But was I fully surrendered? No.

Now that I've surrendered, I feel His presence all the time. Surrendering to God isn't a one-time event. Each day is filled with moments of surrender. When He directs me to do something that may be difficult, and I want to take the easy way out, it requires a moment of surrender.

Trust God

I don't have to wait to go to church on Sunday before I have an encounter with God. I encounter Him numerous times throughout each day. I seek God early when I first wake up. I have a stack of devotional books that I read every morning. Then I sing *Hallelujah*, sing *Jesus Is Lord*, and then I sing *Hallelujah* again. Then I dance for my Bridegroom and continue to give Him glory.

> *The voice of joy, and the voice of gladness, the voice of the bridegroom, and the voice of the bride, the voice of them that shall say, Praise the L*ORD *of hosts: for the L*ORD *is good; for his mercy endureth for ever: and of them that shall bring the sacrifice of praise into the house of the L*ORD*. For I will cause to return the captivity of the land, as at the first, saith the L*ORD*. (Jeremiah 33:11)*

When I finish dancing before the Lord, I continue praising Him for who He is and thanking Him for His abundant blessings. I give Him first place every morning. After I've read His Word, danced before Him, praised Him, and given Him thanks, I then present my petitions to the Father.

I go to my prayer wall and go through every person's name, laying them at the feet of Jesus and interceding for them. Once I pray for those on my prayer wall, I pray for myself. I know that this is my purpose. Each day must start this way to prepare me for whatever tasks God assigns me that day.

"Pray for the peace of Jerusalem."

In the middle of the night, between 2:00 a.m. and 3:00 a.m., God usually awakens me to pray for Israel. I don't know why He has me pray for Israel at that hour of the night. My job is not to question why; my job is to surrender and obey.

I recently checked and found out that when it's between 2:00 a.m. and 3:00 a.m. in the part of the United States where I live, it's between 8:00 a.m. and 9:00 a.m. in Israel. When I'm praying for Israel, they are probably starting their work day. For whatever reason, that's when God wants me to pray.

I'm sure He has others praying at other times of the day and night for His people. The time slot that He has assigned to me happens to be between 2:00 a.m. and 3:00 a.m. God is remarkable!

And I will bless them that bless thee, and curse him that curseth thee: and in thee shall all families of the earth be blessed. (Genesis 12:3)

Pray for the peace of Jerusalem: they shall prosper that love thee. (Psalm 122:6)

"And when I'm old and grey..."

Just because I'm old and my hair is grey doesn't mean I lack value. God is not finished with me. These are fantastic years! I am growing deeper and deeper in love with Jesus, and He is showing me marvelous things.

Now also when I am old and greyheaded, O God, forsake me not; until I have shewed thy strength unto this generation, and thy power to every one that is to come. (Psalm 71:18)

The glory of young men is their strength: and the beauty of old men is the grey head. (Proverbs 20:29)

The hoary (grey) head is a crown of glory, if it be found in the way of righteousness. (Proverbs 16:31)

God has given me a crown of glory, and He said He's going to take care of the greyheaded people. Hallelujah!

"I don't have to figure it out."

Surrendering to God has spiritual benefits, and it also has practical benefits in my

Trust God

daily life. I don't have to figure everything out or be concerned about anything. I give it to the Lord, and He takes excellent care of me.

One example: my hot water tank was making a strange noise. Of course, I did what my husband would have done. I "pulled a Tom." (I'll explain this in a little more detail later.)

I went in and laid hands on the hot water tank and said, "Lord, you know I'm depending on you to provide, to make a way for this to be fixed. You know my financial situation, that I don't have money to fix it."

The following day, my friend Char came over to visit and brought me a St. Patrick's Day dinner of corned beef. Her friend Gary came with her, who is a jack of all trades. (There are no coincidences with God.)

They heard the strange noise my water tank was making, and Gary said, "Let me take a look at it." After checking it he said, "This has to be fixed immediately or your pipes are going to break."

Char and Gary went to the hardware store, Char paid for the part, and when they came back Gary fixed the hot water tank.

The Lord takes care of me, and He does it His way and in His time. Sometimes we think we're casting our care on Him, saying, "Here, I'll give it to you, Lord," but then we try to figure it out and do it our way.

We're either worried that God isn't working fast enough or isn't working things out the way we want. When you cast your cares on the Lord, leave them there. Forget about it. He's taking care of it.

Cast thy burden upon the LORD, and he shall sustain thee: he shall never suffer the righteous to be moved. (Psalm 55:22)

Casting all your care upon him; for he careth for you. (1 Peter 5:7)

Let me explain what I meant when I said I "pulled a Tom." One bitterly cold winter

Trust God

evening, all the water pipes in our house were completely frozen; consequently, we had no water. I looked at my husband and said, "What are you going to do, honey?" He responded, "I'm going to pray."

He knelt down by the tub, put his hand on the faucet, and started praying. All of a sudden, water started flowing freely from the faucet. That was the end of it. We had water. If you work your faith, your faith will work!

When you trust God completely, He will take care of you. He is faithful! When I call on God, He answers every time. He never breaks a promise, and He promises that He will hear us when we call to Him. Tom used to say that Jeremiah 33:3 is God's phone number:

Call unto me, and I will answer thee, and show thee great and mighty things, which thou knowest not.

Chapter Four
Sisters, Friends & Family

I know that I'm not the only one who has ever drunk a cup of sorrow or had family issues. In the Bible, in the book of Genesis, chapters 37, 39, and 40 through 45, we discover that Joseph had <u>major</u> family issues. In a nutshell, chapter 37 describes how Joseph's brothers sold him into slavery, because they were exceedingly jealous of him.

In chapter 39, Joseph is carried off to Egypt as a slave; however, God gave him grace and favor, and he was given a prominent position in Egypt. But then Joseph was falsely accused of a crime and thrown in prison.

A Throwaway Kid

God again prospered Joseph, showed him favor while he was in prison, and put Joseph in charge of all the prisoners.

We see God's vindication of Joseph in chapter 41. Joseph was released from prison and promoted to a major position that was second only to Pharaoh.

From the end of chapter 41 through chapter 45, we learn that a famine spread throughout the land. Joseph's brothers traveled to Egypt to buy food, because that was the sole place where food was available. Not coincidentally, Joseph was in charge of distributing food during the famine.

When Joseph's brothers came to purchase food, they didn't even recognize him, since many years had passed. After several encounters with his brothers, Joseph finally revealed who he was. His brothers were terrified Joseph would punish them for what they had done to him. Joseph, instead, replied in Genesis 50:20:

But as for you, ye thought evil against me; but God meant it unto good, to bring to pass, as it is this day, to save much people alive.

Just like with Joseph, God has taken what was meant for evil against me, and He has turned it to good! God has delivered this "throwaway kid" and surrounded me with a marvelous group of sisters in the Lord and an incredible family.

The Lord has powerfully and dramatically changed my life. Though Satan tried to rob me of family and friends, God has blessed me with more than I could have dreamed was possible.

It's unusual to acknowledge in a book as many people as I will in this chapter; nonetheless, I want to emphasize how God has richly blessed me in the area of family and friends. God is fulfilling His purpose in me, though Satan tried to deprive me of the most precious thing in the universe: love – the love of God and the love of people.

I have innumerable acquaintances, friends, and family from various walks of life. I could fill many more pages, if I wrote about them all. For that reason, I'm going to limit my comments to my immediate family, my sisters who attend the Bible study I host on Thursday evenings, and a few close friends.

In this section about my sisters and friends, I'll share what a blessing these precious ladies are to me and to the Body of Christ, and I'll also share some of our experiences together. They are listed in alphabetical order, because I couldn't possibly list them in order of their importance. I cherish each one for their diverse, distinct personalities.

SISTERS & FRIENDS

Audrey

This beautiful sister is a tremendous blessing to me, and she is a compassionate woman who loves to serve others and bless those around her. Her smile and laughter light up a room. Audrey and her husband, Duane, have enriched my life in many ways. They think nothing of picking me up and taking me places I normally wouldn't be able to go. On several occasions, they've called and asked, "How'd you like to take a road trip?" Or sometimes they'll say, "We'll be there in a few minutes. We're taking you out for dinner." Audrey is an incredible woman of God. There are times she surprises me by showing up at my door with bags of groceries. She does it not because I ask her to; it's because of her love and desire to serve. I thoroughly enjoy the way Audrey exalts God in praise at the Bible studies in my home. Her love for God is openly, unashamedly on display. She is truly inspiring and compels others to dig deep in their spirits to offer God heartfelt praise, rather than simply sing songs.

A Throwaway Kid

BECKY

Becky and I have been sisters in the Lord for a long time. She is a strong Christian woman. My appreciation for our friendship is immeasurable. Becky has three lovely daughters: Emily, Jessica, and Melissa. Her youngest daughter was born on my birthday, which automatically makes her special. I used to watch her girls when they were little. One day, I was carrying the baby, Emily, and I tripped and fell. Nothing happened to the baby, but I skinned my knee. So, I asked Jessica, the middle daughter, "Jessica, can we go in, so you can pray for me?" She said, "No, I'd rather eat."

CHAR

What a dear friend I have in Char. I've known her for many years. Char is very compassionate and generous. On several occasions, when she came to visit, she opened my refrigerator; if she didn't think it was filled properly, she said, "Oh, I've got to take off." She'd leave and return with an

Sisters, Friends & Family

abundance of groceries. I'm blessed to know that she cares that much for me. Char and I have had good times filled with laughter. One afternoon, I was baking a cherry pie. I was busy doing something, and I told Char to take it out of the oven. She lost her grip on it and dropped it on the floor. I said, "You're going to eat this pie, Char!" I took a piece of it and chased after her. She went screaming and ran into the bathroom. I kept chasing after her, and she fell into the tub. But did I stop there? Of course not. I turned on the shower!

Claudia

Claudia is such a dynamo for the Lord. Whenever we get together or talk on the phone, the conversation typically turns to God. She has a hunger and thirst for Him that's contagious. I had the privilege of having Claudia stay with me for a week. I enjoyed her company more than she could know. We prayed together. We laughed together. I truly enjoyed that time with her. I wanted to kidnap her and not let her go home, but I knew she had to get back to her family. She lives about an hour away, and I don't get to see her as much as I'd like. I miss her smiling face, her bubbly personality, and her amazing zeal for God!

CONNIE

Connie is a precious sister in the Lord to me. She's helped me out numerous times. Due to her medical training, I relied on her immensely when Tom had Alzheimer's. She was with me many hours and was a phone call away when I needed someone to listen to me and walk me through the hard times. When I had questions, she had answers for me. She was upfront and told me how long Tom would probably live, and she was right. I told her I didn't want sugar coating. I was adamant that she be honest with me at all times, and I valued her honesty. She delivered honesty with so much love, that I didn't fully feel the sting or pain of that difficult season. The love of Jesus flowed richly through Connie and buffered any overwhelming pain I would've had. She's there when I need her. She doesn't think about herself. She's unselfish with her time and with her love.

GRACE

Grace's actual name is Jean; however, I call her Gracie. We started calling her Gracie, because she was always tripping. She has been there to make sure I have everything I need, whether it's household supplies, food, or taking me to doctor's appointments. When my dryer and refrigerator broke, she took on the responsibility of getting them fixed. If she comes to visit and my refrigerator is empty, she goes to the store and comes back with bags and bags of groceries. Grace is kindhearted, and she loves the Lord!

GRETA

Just thinking about Greta makes me smile. She warms my heart. I admire Greta's commitment to bless her friends and her family. There have been times she has sacrificed her own agenda in order to bless someone else. When Greta and I get together, you can be sure there's going to be laughter. She's one of the sisters I'm not supposed to sit next to in Bible study, because we keep each other laughing. We enjoy our times together. Greta also has a serious side when studying the Scriptures. She has a unique gift of interpreting Scripture in a way that reveals the Bible as an essential instruction manual for practical, everyday living.

JAN

Jan faithfully attends church and several Bible studies throughout the week. I marvel at her hunger for fellowship with other believers in Christ. She likes to surround herself with friends who are rooted and grounded in the Lord. Jan also makes time in her busy schedule to visit a local nursing home every week. I admire and respect her for doing that. I'm sure the nursing home residents look forward to seeing her each

Sisters, Friends & Family

week. Jan is also faithful to commemorate special occasions and birthdays for her friends, whether it be with a phone call, a card, or a gift. Jan is such a blessing to our Bible study. She loves to praise God, study His Word, and talk about the Lord with others. Jan has a way of asking questions in our Bible studies that makes us think about the Word and constrains us to dig deep to find answers to her questions, to dig deeper to find out what God says about things. She also offers valuable input that adds to the study.

JANET

Janet is a friend from Toledo, who is special to me. I don't get to see her as much as I'd like, since she lives about an hour away. She's encouraging and has a knack for making me laugh. Janet sends me cards out of the blue, just to cheer me up. She is a fantastic woman and a valuable sister in the Lord. One afternoon Janet and her husband Larry came to visit me. I was thrilled to see Janet. I hugged her, and we immediately started talking excitedly, as we walked toward the house. As we were walking, she said, "Oh, did you see Larry?" I said, "Oh, is he here?" She said, "Yeah, he's right there." I said nonchalantly, "Oh, hi, Larry," and immediately started right back into our conversation. Janet lost it and starting laughing hysterically. When she sent me a card recently, she signed it, "Janet...and maybe Larry." It was hilarious! Janet and I have a similar sense of humor and relate well together. Once, their cat flipped the lock on the door and locked Larry out of the house. I laughed and asked Janet, "How long did it take you to train that cat?" Without skipping a beat, she replied, "Not as long as you'd think." We frequently go back and forth with one-liners. We were inside my house, getting ready to go for a walk, and it started raining. I asked her, "Do you know what that means, Janet?" She responded, "No, what?" I answered, "The rain is going to shrink us, and we're going to lose weight." She exclaimed, "Let's get going!"

Sisters, Friends & Family

JOSIE

Josie is such a delight! We have been neighbors for many years. Her family has been such a blessing. Since the first time I invited her to come to the Thursday evening Bible studies, she's been faithful to attend. Seeing how she is growing in her walk with the Lord is inspiring. God is strengthening Josie mightily! She has shared miraculous testimonies of how God is working in her life. She has been healed, blessed financially, and so much more! Her excitement about the Bible and the way God is moving in her life is exciting to see. Sometimes, when we're nearing the end of the Bible study and ready to close, she'll say, "Let's read a little bit more. I want to see what happens." It's such a joy to watch her. She brings enthusiasm and curiosity that infuses the whole group with that childlike longing to learn more about our heavenly Father. Josie is like a sponge that soaks up everything concerning Jesus. Her thirst for knowledge of the Word is contagious. She's not shy about her faith. She boldly shares her love of Jesus through social media.

KAREN

Karen is such a fabulous friend and sister in the Lord. As of this writing, I have known Karen for approximately 20 years. When Karen visits, I know I'm in for a laugh. She is quite a character, and I truly enjoy her company. If there's praise music playing, she dances before the Lord and sings praises to Him. She loves to exalt God! Though Karen has her own health issues, she frequently calls or drops by to make sure I'm okay. "Do you need to go anywhere? Can I do anything for you?" she'll ask. "I'll take you wherever you need to go. Do you need to go to the store? Do you need to go to the bank? I'm here for you. I'm a phone call away." At one time, Karen found out that I wasn't eating properly. Her and my friend Sue got together, and they brought in tons of food! I was so blessed! Karen can sense when I need something done or need help. It's like we're on the same wavelength. We are extremely close. Karen is unselfish to a fault. She will go without in order to give to someone in need.

KATHY

Kathy has given me support and confidence. When I'm confused or hurt, she's there for me. She has so much of Jesus flowing out of her that it overflows to other people, and they feel that love. I am grateful for her. When I need someone to talk to, or when I'm feeling down, she gives me the support I need. I value her. She's my sister and my friend.

MARIE

Marie is helpful and freely gives of her time. I really enjoy spending time with her. Because we both have a unique sense of humor, we laugh a lot together. Marie's son, Josh, has the same sweet spirit as his mother. He's very kind and unselfishly gives of his time to help me with things that I need done around the house.

Marcia

My friend Marcia is very faithful and loving. She has always been there for me and is only a phone call away. Whenever I talk to her, she lifts my spirit. She's a thoughtful, kind, and considerate woman.

Pat

Pat is my buddy and my pal. She has such a strong walk with the Lord that it truly blesses me. Pat puts God first and often reminds me, "In the beginning God…" That reminder helps keep me on track and focused on where my priorities should lie. Pat is willing to extend a hand and help anyone in any way she can. She's such a fine example of how to be a servant of God. Pat has wisdom that is invaluable. She has an extraordinary way of telling the truth in such love, that it brings conviction without condemnation. Her heart is tender to what the Holy Spirit is saying to us individually in the Bible study and as a group. The basis of what she shares from the Lord is rooted and

Sisters, Friends & Family

grounded in her love for God and her love for people. When Pat visits throughout the week, I know we're going to end up praying for others and having a conversation centered on the Lord. I look forward to her visits, because I know it will be a time of prayer and a time of laughter.

RITA

What can I say about Rita? If you mention her name, it brings a big old grin to my face, and I automatically begin to laugh. She is such an uplifting sister. She is also able to empathize with others and feel their pain. She is a glowing example of the Bible verse that instructs us to rejoice with those who rejoice and weep with those who weep (Romans 12:15). Rita lives six months in Florida and six months in Ohio. One of Rita's unique attributes is that she has a green thumb and is able to grow lush flowers and plants. Because she is so loving, she gave me a gorgeous coleus plant at the end of one summer before she left for Florida. It was the most gorgeous coleus I have ever seen.

It was tall, thick, and the colors were stunning! When Rita came back from Florida and came to visit me, I sat her down, gave her a box of tissues and said, "You might need these." In short order, I had managed to kill all but a couple of pitiful twigs of the coleus. The look on Rita's face was priceless. She began laughing, buried her head in her hands and kept laughing. Even after the coleus debacle, she still blesses me with plants at the end of each summer. I have noticed, however, that they're getting smaller and smaller. I guess she figures I can't kill the smaller ones. I do, though. I'm really bad with plants; I even killed one of my artificial plants. Rita is the perfect example of grace. At the end of each summer, she graciously blesses me with another plant, although I'm sure she must know it's not going to survive the winter.

Rosa

Rosa is such a pleasant, kind sister. She has a singing voice like an angel. I thoroughly enjoy listening to her, as she praises

God. Rosa is giving, loving, thoughtful, and empathetic. I am truly blessed to have her as my sister in the Lord. A quality I greatly admire in Rosa is that she is family-oriented and is an exceptional example of how to take care of and pray for family. As of this writing, Rosa is a first-time grandmother and is thoroughly enjoying her grandson.

SALLY

Sally is such a beloved friend. She also lives half of the year in Florida and half in Ohio. When she's out of town, she still keeps in touch and keeps me up-to-date on what's happening in her life. I love that she is faithful to call not only me; she calls all her friends to make sure they're okay. Sally has blessed me with sound advice about healthy living. She encourages me to eat nutritious foods and to exercise. She doesn't merely talk the talk. She literally walks the walk. She stopped by one day and said, "Come on, let's go for a walk." Walking around the park with Sally was an enjoyable time of fellowship, as we admired the beauty of God's creation and talked together. Sally goes all out when she blesses her friends. One Saturday she came by to pick me up. When I got in her van, I found out that she had spontaneously picked up two other mutual friends. Sally drove us around, and we spent an enjoyable afternoon in each other's company. There was no pre-planning or agenda. She simply wanted to bless us. We ended up about 30 miles away at a lovely restaurant where we ate dinner together and had a wonderful time. There are not words adequate enough to thank her for what she did that day. It blessed us all greatly!

SHIRLEY

Shirley is such a magnificent blessing to my life! I call her my sweet pea, because she is so precious. Shirley is my living Bible concordance. She has brilliant Bible facts deep in her spirit. Anytime someone has a question, Shirley can cite chapter, verse, context, and cross references. She knows Bible facts, and she can tell you how they apply to practical life. She has such astounding stories to tell and an awesome testimony! As of this writing, Shirley was diagnosed with breast cancer 27 years ago and was told she would not live six months. She is still going strong! She was given another death sentence almost two years ago, as of this writing. She was again told she had six months to live. She's going stronger than ever! Incredibly, Shirley was on hospice for a few months, and they kicked her off, because her health improved greatly. She is a living, breathing testimony of the power of God! She is humble and will tell you she's just a desperate woman running after God. She might consider herself desperate; I think she's one blessed woman of God! Shirley is a treasure trove of information on various topics, including nutrition. Like Sally, Shirley is trying to keep me on the right track. She can tell you which foods heal which conditions, which foods are bad for you, and which foods work well together. I'm trying to follow her advice, because I know first-hand that her diet plan works. I was diagnosed with diabetes and started using Shirley's nutritional regimen. After a couple of months of following Shirley's suggestions, my doctor said that I didn't need diabetes medication and told me to keep doing whatever I was doing. I achieved this outstanding report through prayer and nutrition, not medication. Praise God!

SUE

Sue is a close friend and sister in the Lord. I had the privilege of watching her two cats, Duchess and Miss Kitty, when she had to go on an extended trip. I thoroughly enjoyed having her cats in my home. I am blessed and grateful that she entrusts them to my care. They keep me laughing. The reason Sue travels frequently is because she reaches out to others when they are going through something difficult. I marvel at Sue's heart. She's there for those who are going through trials, to give them a sense of strength, let them know the Lord is there for them, and to encourage them to call on Him. Sue gives unselfishly of herself for the sake

Sisters, Friends & Family

of others. She works for hospice, and she's very special. I do have one minor complaint. The last time I watched her cats, Duchess ate my corned beef sandwich. Not to worry. Sue took me out and bought me a replacement corned beef sandwich. And though Duchess ate my sandwich, she was considerate. She ate all the corned beef and was nice enough to leave me the bread.

ৡৡৡৡৡৡৡ

In summary, I am in absolute awe of how Jesus uses all these sisters and friends as vessels of love. They have amazing hearts and are open to be used by Him. Jesus takes superb care of me, and many times He uses my sisters and friends to bless me. It's fantastic to witness and experience the body of Christ in action!

My sisters in Christ not only talk about the love of God, they demonstrate His love in practical ways. I want to make it clear that my sisters in Christ are dear friends.

They are not merely part of a religious group that gets together once a week to read the Bible. We are genuine friends involved in one another's lives.

MY FAMILY

JOHN SR. & DARLA

From day one, my son, John Sr., has been precious to me. I know that he loves me, and I thank him. As a typical child, he's given me love, laughter, and tears. John lives nearby. All I have to do is let him know I have a need, and he's right there for me. When he met Darla, who is absolutely wonderful, I told her, "I raised him, I spoiled him. I'm giving him to you. No refunds." I raised John well enough to pick someone as beautiful as Darla. She is loving and very good for John. John is soft-spoken. When he comes to visit, he doesn't leave the house without hugging me once or twice and saying, "I love you, Mom." It is a blessing to know that my sons are not afraid to show love.

Sisters, Friends & Family

JIM & JESSICA

My youngest son, Jim, lives about three hours away from me. Although he's not physically near, he is emotionally there for me whenever I need him. In spite of Jim having MS, multiple sclerosis, he still works 60-65 hours per week. Even though he has to drag his leg, it doesn't stop him. When I look at him, I see the part of me that is strength: "I can do it. I'm going to take care of it. I'm going to be fine." Jessica, Jim's wife, sticks by him, and I appreciate her love and devotion to him. We don't get to spend a lot of time together, because of the miles between us. When we all get together, though, we have a really good time.

JOHN JR. & DENISE

I love my grandson, John Jr., dearly. He and his wife, Denise, both love the Lord and have a happy marriage. I tell John Jr., "I will never die, because you have a lot of me in you." John Jr. and Denise attend the same church I do, and we enjoy sitting together and praising God together. I love how John Jr. and Denise stop by my house sometimes and spend the night so that we can spend time together. I admire how John and Denise work hard at their jobs to make a decent life for themselves.

STEVEN & BRITTANY

When my grandson Steven was very young, I ran into a woman in a store, who also had a young grandson. She was going on and on and on, bragging about how smart her grandson was. I said, "I know what you mean. Steven is so smart, he drove himself home from the hospital." Beat that, lady. She couldn't top that one! In all seriousness, Steven and Brittany are such blessings to me. Brittany's exuberance and cheerful personality brighten my day. She is so tenderhearted. When I was sick, she made sure that I had a cup of tea made before she went to work, and she made sure another cup of tea was made when she got home. I'll never forget her thoughtfulness. She is very sensitive and loving. Steven and

Sisters, Friends & Family

Brittany have a beautiful daughter, my great granddaughter, Jasmine, who, in my opinion, is as close to perfection as anyone can be. Jasmine was born before Tom died. I was able to lay her next to Tom, and he was happy to see his great granddaughter. I still have that picture in my mind, as I think of Jasmine lying next to her grandpa, who was bedridden by then. I pray that God will bless Steven, Brittany, and Jasmine above anything they could ever ask or imagine.

Felica

My goddaughter, Felica, blesses me more than mere words can express. She prepares a nutritious dinner for me every day. She wants to make sure that I am well-nourished. Sometimes the food is a little bit too nourishing, if you know what I mean. I get all that green stuff and half the time I've got to ask, "What are we eating? What's this?" "It's good for you, Mom. Eat it," she'll reply. I thank God for Felica and how the Lord has supplied through her. When she stops by daily with dinner, she also makes sure my refrigerator is stocked and that I have everything I need. She recently landscaped my front yard and made it look fantastic! Her deeds demonstrate genuine love in action. I love her so much, and I'm grateful for the Lord's supply through her.

※※※※※※※

Words cannot adequately describe the joy my family brings me. I thank God for blessing me abundantly with their love. I pray that every member of my family will continually walk with God and allow Him to use them for His glory. I look forward to when we will all live with the Lord Jesus Christ in His eternal city, New Jerusalem!

Chapter Five
Be Made Whole

After a tremendously rocky start in life, I finally have a fabulous family and amazing friends! Through their love and the love of God, I have been healed spiritually, emotionally, and physically.

My heart is now open to give love and receive love. The Word of God says in Acts 20:35 *...It is more blessed to give than to receive.* I love giving; it's easy for me. One of the hardest things I've had to learn is how to receive blessings from others, since my formative years were spent fending for myself, and I received love from no one.

I'm slowly learning that when the Lord blesses me, I must gratefully and graciously receive His blessings. He's showing me the importance of receiving His love and the love of others.

I now understand what Jesus meant in Luke 10:27 when He said that the greatest commandments are:

...Thou shalt love the Lord thy God with all thy heart, and with all thy soul, and with all thy strength, and with all thy mind; and thy neighbour as thyself.

The Gospel message is simple: we must love God and love people.

God has miraculously transformed my life through the power of His love! I have finally learned that the secret to receiving His transformative love is to surrender completely to Him.

No matter what you go through, He is with you, watching over you, guiding you through His plan and purpose. He has specifically designed a unique calling for each of His children so that they can help build His kingdom.

When you completely surrender to Him, you have His immeasurable love, peace, and joy. True joy is having Jesus, knowing Him, and walking through life holding His hand.

Joy isn't about a new car, new clothes, or a new house. Some may desire the temporary happiness of wealth. To me, having a relationship with Jesus is true wealth.

When you've got Jesus deep in your heart, the cravings of materialism fade away and you no longer desire frivolous, excessive creature comforts for yourself that are here today and gone tomorrow.

When I think of Jesus, He makes me smile. When I praise Him, I imagine my soul inside with two little feet dancing and going wild, praising the Lord!

I look forward to each morning that I get to dance with my Bridegroom. In the natural, when a couple gets married, at the reception they have that enchanting first dance. I get to experience that first dance every day with my Bridegroom, the Lord Jesus Christ. I love Him so much!

As He did with me, God wants to tell His story through you. He also wants to display His glory and demonstrate His power in you! You can have an intimate relationship with the Creator of the universe, the Giver of life, the Savior of the world, the King above all kings, and the Lord of all!

If you have not accepted Jesus as your Savior, if you have wandered away from Him, or if you have not made Him the Lord of your life by completely surrendering to Him, I invite you to do so by repeating this prayer:

> *Lord Jesus Christ, I confess that I was born a sinner. I ask you to forgive me of my sins. I accept you as my Savior and the Lord of my life. I renounce Satan, and I surrender completely to you. Fill me with your Spirit and empower me to live for you from this day forward. Amen.*

Be Made Whole

I pray that God will bless you and keep you every day of your life, that He will give you favor and provide for you spiritually, physically, and financially. I pray that God will prosper you in your spirit, in your soul, and in your body.

May God bless you in every area of your life and give you His perfect peace, making you whole and complete with nothing missing, nothing lacking, and nothing broken! God bless you now and forever!

Notes

Notes

Notes

Notes

Notes

www.ingramcontent.com/pod-product-compliance
Lightning Source LLC
Chambersburg PA
CBHW060800050426
42449CB00008B/1465